WHERE'S THE MEERKAT? ON HOLIDAY

ILLUSTRATED BY PAUL MORAN, SIMON ECOB
AND WAN (REPRESENTED BY MONKEY FEET)

WRITTEN BY JEN WAINWRIGHT

DESIGNED BY ANGIE ALLISON AND ZOE BRADLEY

Michael O'Mara Books Limited

A Meerkat Adventure

Hi Grandma,

We are all having an amazing holiday. Here are pictures of all the places we have been. Can you spot all ten of us in each picture?

We've made it nice and tricky for you, and we're hiding in the crowds, so you'll need your reading glasses and super-spotting skills to find us.

If you get stuck, we've sent you the answers – they're at the back.

Love the Meerkats

xxx

Grandma Meerkat

Retirement Wing

Sandy Warren

Africa

A Spotter's Guide

A family of mischievous meerkats are having the holiday of a lifetime. All you have to do is spot all ten meerkats in every picture, and tick them off as you find them.

Really eagle-eyed searchers can use the special 'Spotter's Checklists' at the back of the book, where there's more fun stuff to find in every picture and tick off.

Bon voyage and happy searching ...

Meet The Family

Now it's time to meet the meerkats and find out more about the crazy critters in this fantastic family.

From left to right: Samson, Florian, Raoul, Sofia, Albert, Miranda, Maxwell, Matthew, Hannah, Frankie.

Live in:

Sandy Warren, Africa

Like:

Travel, adventure, mischief, fancy dress

Holiday Anthem:

'In The Summertime' – Mongoose Jerry

Travel Essentials:

High fur factor sunscreen, Meerkat Map app, fur straighteners (Sofia)

Holiday Reading:

Our Meerkat In Havana by Graham Greene
The Meerkat In The Hat by Dr Seuss

Favourite Quotation:

'We're all going on a summer holiday' – Cliff Richard

Individual Profiles

Read on to discover more vital information about each member of the family.

Miranda:

Age: 37 (in meerkat years)
Favourite Food: Grasshopper gateau
Dream Destination: A tranquil oasis, or a spa where she could treat herself to a pawdicure
Motto: 'The early meerkat catches the worm'

Florian:

Age: 39 (in meerkat years)
Favourite Food: Toffee sundae with cricket chips
Dream Destination: A bustling city full of different things to see and do
Motto: 'Live, laugh and eat larvae'

Albert:
Age: 69 (in meerkat years)
Favourite Food: Insect paella
Dream Destination: He's happy to go anywhere with his family. As long as there's a comfortable chair ...
Motto: 'Life begins at 60'

Raoul:
Age: 17 (in meerkat years)
Favourite Food: Worm spaghetti with grated grubs
Dream Destination: An extreme adventure getaway, with lots of danger and mud and stuff to climb
Motto: 'Take the antelope by the horns'

Sofia:
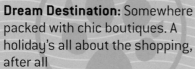
Age: 18 (in meerkat years)
Favourite Food: Baked scorpion with mixed leaf salad
Dream Destination: Somewhere packed with chic boutiques. A holiday's all about the shopping, after all
Motto: 'Beauty is not fur deep'

Matthew:

Age: 13 (in meerkat years)
Favourite Food: Teriyaki termites
Dream Destination: A chocolate factory. Or somewhere with an all-you-can-eat restaurant
Motto: 'A well-fed meerkat is a happy meerkat'

Frankie:

Age: 7 (in meerkat years)
Favourite Food: Cricket casserole
Dream Destination: A theme park with rides and roller coasters and candyfloss and hotdogs and music and fun and giggles. Or a giant dolls house
Motto: 'Play hard and play harder'

Maxwell:

Age: 15 (in meerkat years)
Favourite Food: Stir-fried spiders
Dream Destination: The future. If only he could build a time machine ...
Motto: 'The sky's the limit (unless there's a falcon around)'

Samson:

Age: 20 (in meerkat years)
Favourite Food: Grubs on toast
Dream Destination: A tropical rainforest, full of beautiful plants and flowers
Motto: 'Don't follow the beaten path. Go your own way and leave a termite trail'

Hannah:

Age: 11 (in meerkat years)
Favourite Food: Ant larvae pie
Dream Destination: Somewhere with a big pool to splash around in all day long
Motto: 'Make your dreams as big as an elephant'

FLIGHTS

LHZ62 Düsseldorf	A11
AB819 Zurich	C4
LDZ60 London	B4
LHZ06 Frankfurt	B1
SN258 Brussels	A4
LH303 Stuttgart	A3
AT403 Athens	C3

5

FLIGHTS

LHZ62 Düsseldorf	A11
AB819 Zurich	C4
LDZ60 London	B4
LHZ06 Frankfurt	B1
SN258 Brussels	A4
LH303 Stuttgart	A3
AT403 Athens	C3

At The Airport

The meerkats are twiddling their thumbs at baggage reclaim, waiting for their cases. It's not just the kids who are excited, Miranda and Albert are practically jumping up and down, too. They can't wait for their holiday to get started.

Maxwell has to be held back from clambering on to the luggage conveyor belt. He wants to ride the belt and check out where all the bags go once they disappear from view!

Tick off all ten meerkats as you find them.

Checking In

Now the fun can really start. The family
has arrived at their luxurious hotel,
and they're about to get settled in.

Matthew has been teasing Frankie and
Hannah that they'll have to sleep in bunk
beds because they're the youngest.
Frankie's on the point of having a bit of
a tantrum, but when she's shown to her
room and sees the ENORMOUS soft bed,
and chocolates on the pillows,
she soon cheers up.

Tick off all ten meerkats as you find them.

At The Beach

The meerkats love to be beside the sea. Whether they're sunbathing, paddling or paragliding – a day at the beach is sure to keep everyone happy.

Albert is feeling wonderfully relaxed. He has been floating in the sea and listening to the sound of the waves and the steel band, but now he's ready for some action. He has spotted a limbo contest on the sand. He's confident that he can impress the ladies and walk away a winner. Who says you can't teach an old meerkat new tricks?

Mountain Biking

When the girls were promised a scenic bike ride, this was definitely not what they had in mind. Everywhere they look there are spinning wheels and whirring pedals.

Frankie's terrified of cycling. She's still a real beginner, and only had the stabilisers taken off her bike back at the warren last month. She may be scared, but she refuses to be left behind. As the family race off, Frankie pedals hard to keep up. There are some wobbles and a couple of skids, but as she crosses the finish line she feels really proud of herself.

Festival Fever

After much begging and pleading, Raoul has convinced everyone to come to a music festival and watch some of his favourite bands take to the stage.

He has been worrying that he hasn't packed wellies, but he's in luck. The sun is shining, the music pumping, the burgers frying, and, despite Miranda's seriously embarrassing dance moves, Raoul's having a great time.

After the band finish their set, he plans to try and sneak into the VIP tent to get some autographs.

A Camping Trip

The meerkats regularly sleep out under the stars back at the warren, so this camping trip makes them feel right at home.

The idea of toasting marshmallows is completely new though, and the whole family thinks it's a genius idea. Soon they're having a contest to see who can fit the most marshmallows into their mouth at once. Miranda plans to stock up on the sweet, fluffy treats and is thrilled at the thought of showing off to the neighbours back home. She'll seem so exotic and sophisticated!

At The Station

The train has arrived to take the meerkats to their next exciting holiday destination, but there's time for some fun at the station before they go.

While Albert refuses to stop watching the clock, in case the train leaves without them, Samson and Sofia are enjoying some people-watching. Samson loves watching families together, seeing how excited the children are. For Sofia, it's all about the outfits. She's horrified by what some people are wearing, and is very glad she has packed enough to stay chic at all times.

Whale Watching

The family are on a once-in-a-lifetime trip to spot whales in the freezing ocean.

Hannah is gobsmacked. She thought the elephants back home in Africa were big, but these beautiful sea creatures are absolutely ENORMOUS. She loves how graceful they are, as they dive and splash their huge tails.

Little Frankie is more interested in the penguins waddling around on the ice. She has the rest of the family in stitches as she perfects her penguin impression.

A Firework Display

As soon as the meerkat family arrives in the park, the kids scamper off and disappear in the crowd.

Miranda knows she should be looking for her unruly children, but she's looking up at the skies, and every time there's an explosion of sparkles, she ooohs and aaaahs along with everyone else.

She's sure the kids will be just as fascinated by the fireworks as she is. So wherever they are, they can't be getting into that much trouble ... right?

Ice Skating

At home, Albert adores watching 'Mongooses on Ice' on the TV. He has always wanted to try his hand at skating, but now he's feeling a little nervous. He has seen Matthew limp off the ice in a sulk after a failed attempt at a loop jump, and even Sofia is looking a bit wobbly on her paws.

Albert's certain that he'll pluck up the courage to get on the ice and show them all how it's done a bit later. Right now he's concentrating on finishing the crossword, and his third mug of cocoa.

□ □ □ □ □ □ □ □ □ □

At The Museum

The children weren't particularly keen to visit the museum today, but now they're having a great time.

Raoul loves the dinosaur skeletons – he thinks he'd make a pretty fearsome predator if he'd been alive in prehistoric times. Samson prefers the Viking longship. He's a big fan of the carved figurehead, and can picture himself as a fierce warrior on the high seas, with the wind in his fur. He reckons Vikings never had to do homework or suffer teasing by their little brothers.

Sightseeing

Today the family are off to see some of the city's most famous attractions. From old buildings and beautiful squares, to famous movie locations and trendy boutiques – today's the day to see it all.

Florian is most excited about the open-topped tour bus that will take them from site to site. He's fought his way to the front on the top deck, and has been taking pictures of himself sitting proudly in the front seat. While Sofia would prefer a limo, for Florian this really is the only way to travel!

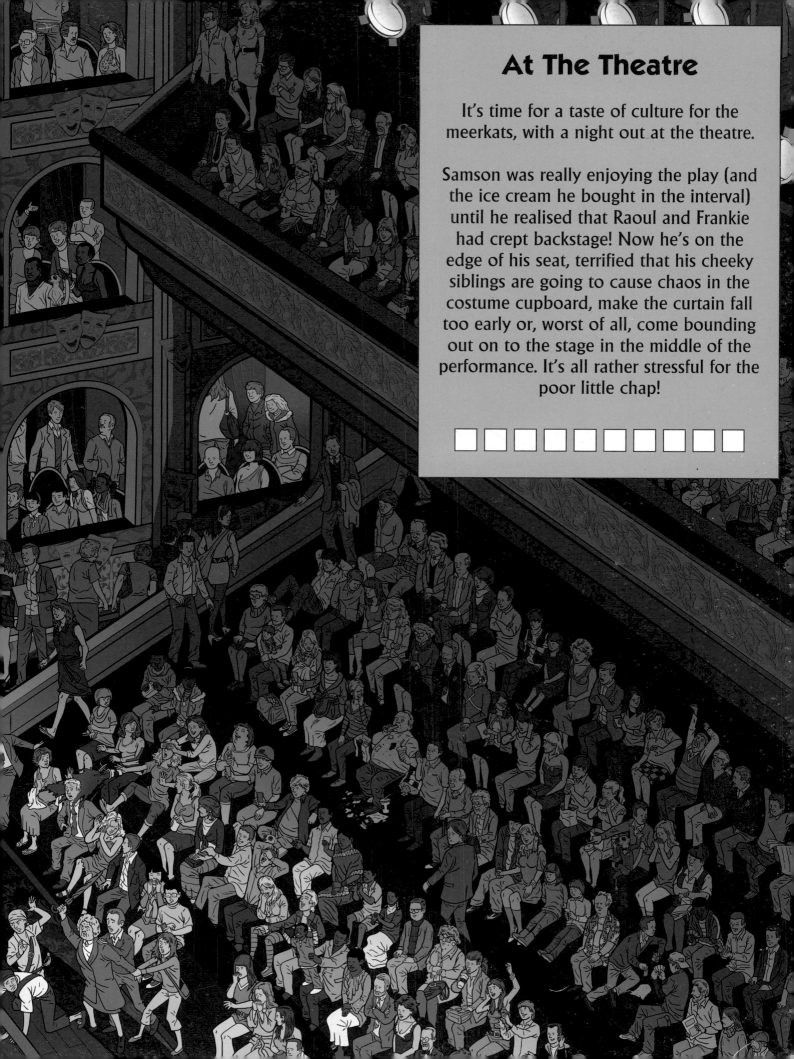

At The Theatre

It's time for a taste of culture for the meerkats, with a night out at the theatre.

Samson was really enjoying the play (and the ice cream he bought in the interval) until he realised that Raoul and Frankie had crept backstage! Now he's on the edge of his seat, terrified that his cheeky siblings are going to cause chaos in the costume cupboard, make the curtain fall too early or, worst of all, come bounding out on to the stage in the middle of the performance. It's all rather stressful for the poor little chap!

By The Pool

It's a roasting hot morning, and the family's having a splashing day by the pool.

Sofia and Miranda have slicked their fur with sunscreen and draped their towels over the best sun loungers, where they plan to stay for several hours.

Maxwell is flinging things into the pool and making Samson dive to get them. Matthew has gone down the slides 30 times and shows no sign of stopping, and Florian is battling his fear of heights, and psyching himself up to dive off the high board.

At The Zoo

The family's arrival at the zoo is causing a bit of a stir. There's a feeling of excitement in the air in all of the animal enclosures, and it's not just the apes who are monkeying around.

The meerkats are confused by the fuss people seem to be making around them. Albert is getting pretty fed up with people taking photos of him and cooing over how cute he looks in his shorts. Sofia, on the other hand, is in heaven and ready for her close-up. She feels her inner celebrity has finally been recognised.

Whitewater Rafting

Much to everyone's surprise, it was Hannah who suggested this daredevil day out. She's decided to be a bit braver, and now there's no stopping her as she dodges rocks and whirling rapids in her cute orange life jacket.

Not wanting to be outdone by his little sister, Raoul leapt into his boat and paddled off at top speed, but he's now wishing he'd paid more attention to the instructors. There's a really big drop coming up, and those rocks don't look very friendly ... GULP!

Theme Park Time

Frankie and Florian were both completely unable to sleep last night. They just love theme parks, and the excitement kept them wide awake. Now, they're running from ride to ride, whooping and shrieking as they go.

Maxwell said he would rather while away the hours in front of his computer, but after his fifth stick of candyfloss, he's beginning to see what all the fuss is about. Soon enough, he's at the front of the queue for the biggest ride of them all, 'The Super Looper'.

Answers

Spotter's Checklist

- A monkey-shaped package
- A man with a mop
- A woman holding pink flowers
- A man proposing to his girlfriend
- A plane spotter
- A child in a red cap
- A girl with a big teddy bear
- Three no entry signs
- A purple suitcase
- A woman eating an apple

AT THE AIRPORT

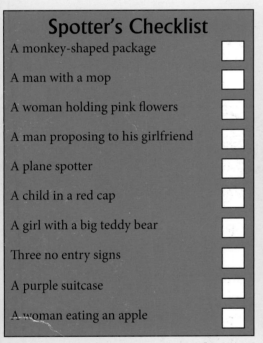

CHECKING IN

Spotter's Checklist

- Someone building a house of cards
- A man on a tiny bike
- A woman doing the vacuuming
- A child drawing on hotel property
- A man with a guitar case
- Someone yelling at the hotel manager
- Someone riding on a hotel trolley
- A waiter with a bottle of champagne
- A man playing the violin
- A child standing on a chair

Spotter's Checklist

AT THE BEACH

Someone playing Frisbee

A man with a harpoon

Someone with a sore head

A limbo contest

A woman with a tattoo

Kids building a sandcastle

A boy with a fishing net

A man in a red, green and yellow hat

A purple and yellow stripy swimsuit

A woman talking on the phone

Spotter's Checklist

A barefoot spectator

Two people clinging on for dear life

A boy on his father's shoulders

A rider in a frog costume

A girl wringing out her T-shirt

A bright pink bike

A water fight

A man doing a wheelie

Someone being pulled out of the water

A man carrying his bike

MOUNTAIN BIKING

FESTIVAL FEVER

Spotter's Checklist

Four burly bodyguards

Someone being sick

Two crowd surfers

A group of fairies

A man signing autographs

Roadies playing cards

A tray of burgers

A red and white flag

A man in a purple tie-dyed shirt

A girl in ripped jeans

A CAMPING TRIP

Spotter's Checklist

A sleeping-bag sack race ☐

Two dogs fighting ☐

A man juggling with fire ☐

A boy scaring his friends ☐

Someone fixing a van ☐

A man climbing a tree ☐

Someone playing the banjo ☐

A telescope ☐

A man telling a ghost story ☐

Marshmallows being toasted ☐

Spotter's Checklist

A man falling over on the stairs ☐

A woman carrying a stack of presents ☐

A couple arguing ☐

A girl with pink hair ☐

A boy playing with a toy train ☐

Two people eating ice cream ☐

A man on a bike ☐

A woman running ☐

Two people sliding down the banisters ☐

Someone carrying a skateboard ☐

AT THE STATION

WHALE WATCHING

Spotter's Checklist

A couple being pooed on by gulls ☐

A man in an eyepatch ☐

A penguin driving ☐

A man with a TV camera ☐

Someone being chased by penguins ☐

Someone holding a fish ☐

A snowboarder ☐

Four pairs of binoculars ☐

A cluster of barnacles ☐

Someone having trouble with boxes ☐

Spotter's Checklist

A smiley-face poster ☐

A child upside down ☐

A woman carrying a puppy ☐

Five firefighters ☐

A couple with a picnic basket ☐

A woman with pink flowers ☐

Kids with sparklers ☐

A man with a double bass ☐

A girl on a scooter ☐

A man with a guitar on his back ☐

A FIREWORK DISPLAY

Spotter's Checklist

A child learning to play ice hockey ☐

A man in a top hat ☐

Girls sitting on the edge of the rink ☐

A family not wearing skates on the ice ☐

A snowman ☐

A child on a sledge ☐

A man doing a splits jump ☐

A girl helping her friend up ☐

Someone falling down in an orange scarf and a green top ☐

A chain of skaters ☐

ICE SKATING

AT THE MUSEUM

Spotter's Checklist

Two men pretending to be aeroplanes ☐

Someone doing a bear impression ☐

A boy in a tribal mask ☐

A professor with a pipe ☐

A stray cat ☐

A burglar ☐

A boy with a fizzy drink ☐

A child frightened by a tortoise ☐

An old couple reading a map ☐

A man on his laptop ☐

Spotter's Checklist

SIGHTSEEING

A boy climbing where he shouldn't

A clown

A man with a baguette

A thief

Three human statues

Some dropped shopping

A man on roller skates

A man eating a banana

A T-shirt with a target sign

A man on a box giving a speech

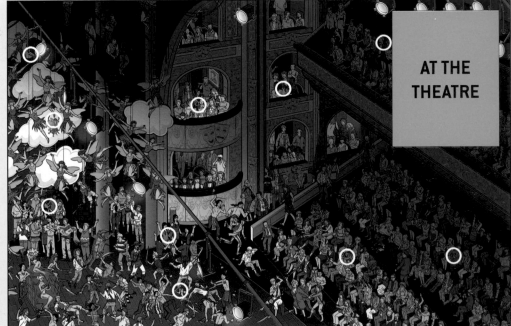

Spotter's Checklist

AT THE THEATRE

An actor holding his wig

A mermaid in love

A cold drink being spilled

A man eating messily

An angry old lady

An old man yawning and stretching

Boys playing cards

A girl blowing bubblegum bubbles

A woman covering her ears

A tiny baby

Spotter's Checklist

BY THE POOL

Someone fully clothed being pushed in

A woman wearing a sombrero

A man in armbands

A boy with a waterpistol

A man doing butterfly stroke

A pink swimming cap

A human pyramid

An inflatable duck

Two men wearing necklaces

A sunbather having water poured on her

Spotter's Checklist

AT THE ZOO

- Three escaped monkeys
- A stinky wheelbarrow
- An elephant being fed a banana
- A boy losing his cap
- A girl wearing a black beret
- A man in a Hawaiian shirt
- A boy on his father's shoulders
- The odd cat out in the lion enclosure
- Six zookeepers
- A peacock

Spotter's Checklist

- A woman meditating
- Three sharks
- A baseball glove
- A man scuba diving
- Three girls jumping into the river
- A horse
- Two men abseiling
- Someone reading the newspaper
- A purple kite
- Four balloons

WHITEWATER RAFTING

THEME PARK TIME

Spotter's Checklist

- A man going backwards on a ride
- Two conga lines
- A stallholder having a bad day
- A heart-shaped balloon
- A fortune teller with a crystal ball
- A really spooked man
- A woman with four ice creams
- Two toy tigers
- An enormous bag of candyfloss
- A man slipping over

Published in Great Britain in 2012 by Michael O'Mara Books Limited,
9 Lion Yard, Tremadoc Road, London SW4 7NQ

www.mombooks.com

Copyright © Michael O'Mara Books Limited 2012

A CIP catalogue record for this book is available from the British Library.

Hardback ISBN: 978–1–84317–952–8
Paperback ISBN: 978–1–84317–889–7

1 3 5 7 9 10 8 6 4 2

This book was printed in May 2012 by L.E.G.O., Viale dell'Industria 2, 36100, Vicenza, Italy.

Papers used by Michael O'Mara Books are natural, recyclable products made from wood grown in sustainable forests. The manufacturing processes conform to the environmental regulations of the country of origin.